BETTER LIGHT A CANDLE

Better light a candle than curse the darkness
CHINESE PROVERB

David Lorimer

First published in paperback in 2022

ISBN 979 10 415 0569 2

Typeset in Minion 9.5/14.5pt
by The Foundry, Edinburgh

For Marianne, who has deeply inspired me with her inner and outer beauty.

CONTENTS

PREFACE

Wordsworth famously said that poetry is the breath and finer spirit of knowledge. Poetry uses language descriptively and evocatively, enabling the poet to convey a concentrated meaning that might take many pages of prose to express. As such, it embodies the poet's core philosophy and outlook in a few pages.

My love of poetry goes back to my time in the 1970s of the University of St Andrews, where my tutor in French poetry was the inspiring and enthusiastic Ian Higgins. He taught us Baudelaire, Verlaine, Rimbaud, Mallarmé, Valéry and Francis Ponge. I even wrote a few poems in French as a result. My friend Charles Maclean introduced to me to Ted Hughes, and gave me a subscription to the Poetry Book Society for my 21st. More recently, the poet who speaks most directly to me is David Whyte.

For many years I wrote very little poetry, and this collection dates from the last eight years. The influence of T.S. Eliot's *Four Quartets* will be apparent, and also that of Goethe and Hermann Hesse, which I read in German.

Sainte Colombe-sur-l'Hers,
July 2022

BEING TOGETHER

Being together
Being
Together,
Present
To each other,
In each other,
Silently flowing
Between our being
Entwined in love.
Squeezing gently
Together,
Closer than our own
Beating hearts.
We are one
Being together.

Still waters run deep in my heart
Resting softly in the Centre
Waiting,
Suspended,
Merged into Oneness.

Breathing slowly in and out
The rhythm of Life
Almost imperceptible
Flows in close embrace.

My soul's vibrating note
Exquisitely tuned
Reaches into your beautiful presence,
Shimmering gently,
Touching you tenderly
With love and light.

THE CLOAK OF LOVE

Arms entwined,
Enfolded and enfolding,
We gently move
In the slow harmony of love.

Showers of shimmering stars
Cascade and sprinkle
Down our spines.

Then softly enveloping us
In velvet darkness,
The cloak of love
Protects those precious places,
Safely opening
The innermost recesses
Of our hearts.

THE SPACE BETWEEN

Between
The space
Between us
Is only love,
Between
Two beings
As one
Flow of life,
Together.

WEAVING

Weaving you
A scarlet gown
Enfolding you tenderly
In love,
Protecting your heart,
A sensitive bird
Softly nestling inside,
A warm bundle
That yet
Longs for freedom
To fly away,
Soaring,
Swooping,
Diving
From mountain to lake
Then returning home again
To the nest
And cosily cuddling up
Together.

THE HEART SPEAKS

Le coeur a ses raisons que la raison ne connaît point (the heart has its reasons of which reason is utterly unaware)

BLAISE PASCAL

The mind
Weighs,
Ponders,
Plans,
Worries,
Doubts and fears,
Even decides, but
Swaying back and forth

While the heart
Has its own reasons
To calm the vacillating mind,
Suffusing the depths
To reach the still centre,
Then scattering doubt,
Clearly feeling
Love
Welling up,
Overflowing
Into life
Together.

OPENING UP

Light seeps through
Cracks in the tender heart,
Melting resistance
Into the fire of love,
Opening up a vulnerable space
For flowers to bloom
And wave in the wind
Together.

WOUNDED

Wounded,
Balanced
On the knife-edge of hope
On the cliff-edge of despair
Where life is precarious
But precious.

The candle of hope
Extinguished
By despair,
Powerless.

The flame of hope
Rekindled
By vision
By engagement
By passion
By love
By courage
By faith
In the future,
In new possibilities

But still on the knife-edge
Still on the cliff-edge
Poised,
Still wounded
By human suffering

Yet
Celebrating
The beauty of life
Together.

This poem was written at the Tamera Community in Portugal (www.tamera.org). It seeks to evoke the alternating moods of activists engaged in action but sometimes feeling powerless in the face of massive destructive drivers of global deterioration. Activists must nevertheless keep faith with their vision for the future despite setbacks.

WHY ON EARTH?

Why on Earth
Are we here?
Why on Earth?
Why Earth?
On Earth?
In Earth
Planted as a seed
To grow
To bloom
To fruit,
Embodying
Polarity
Seeking
To connect
Intimately
In union
In communion
In loving embrace
Together.

ESSENCE

For Richard Griffith-Jones (1949–2018)

To see and to be seen
To hear and to be heard
To open and to be opened
To be touched and to touch
To be loved and to love,
This
Is the fruit of light distilled,
The woven texture,
The feel,
The taste,
The priceless currency
Of life
Together.

My friendship with Richard endured over 50 years, from school through university and thereafter. He was the kindest and most considerate of people and greatly loved by his many friends – 600 people turned out at his funeral. This poem is a reflection on what we can distil out of our life experience – we can only take what we are and have become in terms of being when we ourselves cross the threshold into the next life.

ANGLES OF APPROACH

Speaking words
Swooping swallows
Cut through as
Life in motion,
Chirping not talking,
Being joy
Flying freely
Through the air,
Perching above
Looking down
On chattering minds
Longing to be steeped
In deep silence.

This poem was written during a talk at the wonderful Science and Non-Duality (SAND) conference at Titignano Castle in Italy in July 2018. I was struck by the swallows flying in the rafters while the lecture was going on . . .

STILL MOVING

We must be still and still moving
Into another intensity
For a further union, a deeper communion . . .

T.S. ELIOT,
Four Quartets, 'East Coker'

Still moving,
Suspended
In stillness,
The mind calm
Rippling only gently,
A cloud of thought
Passing slowly through,
Mirrored only lightly,
A wisp of smoke
Dispersing,
Dissipating
Finely in the clear air,
The lightest brushstroke,
A white feather
Alighting,
Floating,
Flowing
Gently away.

In the summer of 2019, we walked a section of the Sentier Cathare between Puivert and Foix with a couple of friends. We used TS Eliot's Four Quartets *to accompany us on this journey, so these lines were still resonating a few weeks later.*

GREAT ENDINGS

Autumn rains weep
Down sodden branches
Sweeping away falling leaves.
Only desolation remains,
A solitary tree
Stripped,
Blasted,
Tears streaming down.

Standing in the fire of grief
Consumed by flames of love and loss,
Leaping into the unknown
Drawn by a silver thread
Fragile and vulnerable
Yet enfolded,
Nested in appreciation for life,
Unfolding a bud of hope,
Sensing the precious presence of beauty,
A healing path
Beyond the open wound.

I was touched by Diana Percy's presentation at SAND Italy on beautiful endings as opportunities for new beginnings if we have the courage to engage consciously and grow towards healing ourselves and others through suffering and bereavement.

SNOWFLAKE LEAVES

Crystal frost
Grips
The autumn trees,
Acacias
Releasing leaves
Like snowflakes
Onto the flowing river,
Floating downstream
Then sinking
Transparently,
Entering into
The cycle of life.

We live next to the River Hers and walk along it every morning – this poem reflects a striking experience in the life-cycle of leaves.

CORK

Standing
Stripped
Of protection,
Yet still
Rooted
In Earth
In Life
To regrow.

Meanwhile
Compressed
Transformed
Released
Into celebration.

Tamera, May 2019 – I went for a walk and stood for a few minutes in front of a cork tree stripped of its bark, an emblem of generosity and resilience. And as a student, I spent a number of months working for the champagne house Moet et Chandon, where I found out something about nature of the cork and discovered the surprising fact that its shape is cylindrical before being squeezed into the bottle.

FIRE AND ROSE

Split
Through the heart,
Renouncing
Eros,
Battling for Agape
Against the energy of nature
Projecting
Without hope.

Yet
Longing for union,
Expressing movement
Through dance,
The energy of Nature
Courses through life,
Growing flowers
Kissed by the sun,
Embracing
The Earth
Awakening
Love and joy within.

STUCK

Desire
Stone cold,
Wedged in a cleft
Of numb resistance,
Excluding support
By exclusion.

Past patterns
Press in,
Preventing movement;
A grinding halt
Sinking further down,
A heavy load
To bear in the dark
With joy and birdsong
All around.

Waiting for the sky to open up
For new shoots to sprout
Out of the frozen ground.

I WANT DOESN'T GET – A CHILDHOOD MAXIM

So no desires
No demands
No feelings
No expectations:
Avoid disappointment.

If you disobey
You will be punished . . .
You don't deserve

Anything.

Defending isolation
As independence,
Restraint
As modesty,
The river of life runs dry.
Undesirable,
Desiccated,
Closed off from contact,
Disconnected from support.

In time, maybe
The snake can stir in the darkness
The juice can begin to flow
Freely into the light.

THE KEYBOARD OF LIFE

Prelude in C sharp minor, Book 2, 48
Preludes and Fugues by JS Bach

For Rosalyn Tureck

A delicate touch
Of sensitive sadness,
The space
Between
The notes of experience
Passing softly
Through a flowing
Robe of light.

Nostalgic ripples,
Timeless realms
Seeping sequentially
Into time,
A subtle beauty
Almost imperceptible
Lightly brushing the ear,
Exquisite tenderness
Deeply touching
The heart.

I am listening to the great Rosalyn Tureck as I edit these poems. She was the foremost performer of Bach in her day and I had the privilege of hearing her live in both London and Paris. On the cover of her Goldberg Variations she writes: 'I do not play these as a virtuoso performance but rather as a life experience. For me, listening to Bach reformats my mind with order, fluidity and beauty.'

THE SERPENT AND THE CROSS

For Helena and Rachel

Rising waters,
Swirling eddies
Swallow up
The floating cross,
Sweeping away
Crumbling and corrupted
Structures
Of power and sin.

Swimming serpents sinuously
Slide and coil around
This sinking cross,
Sensuously surfacing
Centuries of shame and guilt.

Lovers entwined
Innocently alight
On fresh soil,
Eros and Agape
Conjoined,
Reaching into
The heart of the world.

A purple opening hand
Unfurling innocent gestures
Of pure beauty.

Here and now,
The thinnest thread
Suspends
A tiny bobbing pod
Exquisitely
Wavering in the wind.

Clover

Slow motion
Firework
Of white light
Enclosing sweet nectar
Within a threefold fractal.

At Home

Sixfold pink
Perched on a tall stem,
Tiny insects
Crawl in safely
For shelter and food
Amid the yellow stamens.

GRASPING (1)

Fine green tendrils
Firmly grasp
The vertical grass head
Onto a horizontal plane.

EMBRACE (2)

Fine green tendrils
Twine around the grass head
Tightly clasping together.

Two ways of seeing the same natural process.

THE SOURCE OF TOGETHERNESS

'Love is not a private pleasure,
but a gift to the world'

DIETER DUHM

The source of togetherness
Is not what you think,
Your task is to find it.

Setting out on an arduous search,
The lost soul of fulfilment
In another,
The quest is fruitless.

Returning home
Armoured with fear,
The way is barred
The door is locked.

So start again.

This time the journey is within,
Giving and receiving
Without fear,
Naked being

Open
Exposed
Surrendered.
Yet strongly anchored inside.
Only now can the other come close,
Closer still,
Touching the tender heart of love
Together.

A priceless blessing from life
A precious gift to the world.

SPIRALLING IN AND OUT

Opening
Awakening
Arising
Remembering
Our Source.

Unfolding love,
Nurturing trust,
Connecting hearts
In freedom.

Shining beads of light
Threading together
A shimmering necklace,
A sparkling field
Of close community.

Strange attractor
Magnetising,
Constellating
Healing gems
Spiralling out
In a wounded world
Crying out
For contact and compassion.

A world enfolded
In the womb of life
Awaiting a sacred sunrise,
A rising star emerging,
Radiating its rhythmic power
On a parched and yearning Earth.

CODA

Life unfolds naturally in its own rhythm and time

LIVING WATERS

Truth flows forth
Pure
From deep underground,
Quenching spiritual thirst
In arid times.

The painted chapel
Broods
Over the running waters
Channelling
Fluid spirals
Into fixed ideas.

The sacred planes
Bend protectively overhead,
Strongly rooted
In the past
Though living
In silent presence,
Witnessing
Our slow but steady transformation.

I wrote this poem after walking to a chapel from an old monastery near Plovdiv in Bulgaria.

Core
Coeur
Care
Chor
Courage
Communion
Choir
Courting
Counting
Connecting
Together.

STRIVING

Es strebt der Mensch solang er lebt
(Humans strive for as long as they live)
GOETHE, *Faust* II

Seeking,
Striving,
Swirling
Movement of the mind
Grasping,
Defining,
Planning,
Not being.

The flower simply
Opens,
Blooms,
Closes into fruit,
Seeding notes
Dropping into
Still water
Rippling away
In rhythm
And coming
Finally to rest.

FRANTIC ANTICS

Rushing across the page
On a mission,
The proactive ant
Hurries along,
Never stops,
The to-do list
Ever lengthening,
Frantic multitasking
Gets there in the end –
Or does it?

Pausing momentarily
Only to restart –
The beat of frenetic activity
Busy
Then suddenly
Drained,
Exhausted,
Spent – time
Accounted for
But maybe lost.

RADIANCE

Golden crystals
Sprinkle,
Sparkle
Ever so subtly,
A fine shower
Cascading softly down
Into the opening heart,
Blessing the Earth
With a warm blanket of love.

Tread lightly,
Breathe gently
In this hallowed space,
Knowing,
Touching,
Feeling into
The tender radiance of love.

ARBUTUS PENDING

Strong roots
Stretch into
Overhanging earth.
A clenching fist
Opens up
To fine limbs
Reaching into the sky
But stripped of bark,
Clinging precariously
To life,
Boldly defying erosion,
Staving off gravity and death.
Rooted in stillness
We too stretch into
Space and time,
Releasing a ripple of joy
Onto the shimmering waters
Of life.

ALCHEMY

I intended
never to grow old
but the temple bell sounded – Jokun

In the autumn of life
green turns to gold,
grapes pressed into wine,
wine distilled into the fire of spirit
forging crystal diamonds of wisdom,
the fruitful treasure
of fully ripened love.

A FINAL BLAZE

A luminous leaf
waves and flutters
to the ground,
a final blaze,
a fragile wisp
of transient beauty,
yet protecting the earth
with waiting bulbs beneath.

I wrote these poems after visiting a Japanese Memorial Garden on Cascadia Island.

ALL IN THE SAME CANOE

Crafted
From living trees
In ancient forests
Tended
By countless generations
Rooted
In earth,
Connecting,
Caring,
Communing
Together.

Offering
To share
With open hearts,
Paddling
In the same canoe
Together.

Then –
Abruptly
Felled,
Cleared,
Extracted,
Rooted out
By grabbers

Converting
Verbs to nouns,
Trees to lumber,
Minds to closed beliefs.

So certain in intent
The rugged man
Paddles
His own canoe
Alone.
Striving so hard
To win the race,
Tenacious to the last
He finally falters,
Nature exhausted.

A daunting insight
Slowly dawns –
We're all
In the same
Canoe
Together.

This poem was inspired by a visit to the Parliament and Museum in Victoria, British Columbia – the very names of the city and province conjure up its colonial past so devastating to the First Nations. Only now are we coming to a fuller realisation of this cultural genocide and the importance of indigenous ways of knowing and being in Nature.

A DAISY IN JANUARY

A solitary daisy
Resplendent
Outstretched,
A tiny living presence
In a vast open field.
Not another flower in sight.

Amazed,
I ask myself:
Is it the first,
Or the last?
Does it even matter?

As I write at night
By the cosy fire,
The daisy will be closed
Under the chill light of the moon,
Only to open again at sunrise,
A promise of life renewed
In midwinter.

THE DANCING BREATH OF LIFE

Ocean tides rise and fall
As moon breathes long;
Trees slowly unfurl their leaves
Into softly warming air,
Exhaling scented blooms
Mostly unremarked,
Noticed only
By watchful beings
Inhaling deeply,
Drinking beauty in,
A nectar moment
Dancing deftly
With the blissful breath of life.

Gliding chains of dancers
Entwined as one breathing being
Sway in swinging rhythm,
Flowing to and fro
Circling towards and away,
Uniting and dividing,
Breathing in,
Breathing out,
Constellating archetypal patterns
Inside ancient sacred space,
Merging briefly together
To celebrate
The Oneness of Life.

YELLOW BUTTERFLY

Hatched out,
Stumbling into
Premature warmth
Between winter and spring,
A yellow butterfly
Exalts in the moment,
Fanning out its wings
Into the azure sky.

The cool evening
Brings sleep,
A deeper hibernation.
Wings closed in prayer,
The butterfly awaits
The next warm breeze
To open up once more,
To flutter free
In radiant light.

OPEN TO RECEIVE

Are you open to receive
Or tightly clenched,
Defending yourself against life,
Locked down
In fearful apprehension?

When just outside
The spring sun shines
Strongly down
On blackthorn blossom branches,
Steadily opening
Each flower in turn –
Five white petals stretched out
Towards the light
Expectantly await
The roving bee's awakening kiss.

Are you too ready to receive,
Opening from within,
Reaching out
To give, to share a blessing,
Surrendering fear,
Touching one another,
Holding close together
In this one precious present moment?

BREATHE IN SPACE

Breathing
Space
Between the lines
Of sand
Rippling away
Into the shimmering sea.

Receding tides
Breathe in
Rhythmically,
Relaxing waves out
Over vast ocean horizons.

Deep release
Pressures
Drop away,
The slow night air
Wafts and billows
In still night calm;
Light from long ago,
Those countless glistening stars
Stand in silent witness to
Our present lives on Earth
From distant cycles past.

At dawn a crystal dew
Alights
Inside the yearning heart –
A breathing space
For inner peace
At last.

ON HOLD

Holed up,
We hold out
For hope –
Just holding on
While holding off
Despair,
Holding back
Fear,
Yet
Holding in our hands
The longed-for
Beating heart
Of tender love
We hold so dear.

EASTER ORCHID

Stem shoots
Straight up,
Emerging reborn
From the dark
And fecund womb
Of moist earth.

Enfolded life
Spirals out
From the centre,
Unfolding
Intricate patterns
Of purple beauty
Into time and space.

Expanding ecstasy
Reaches out
In fullness of being . . .
Only
To contract again
To circle round,
Refolding back
Into the tomb of earth.

We too sleep and wake
Forgetting and remembering,
Dying and rising again,
Our souls ascend
As crystal radiance,
Intimately interlaced,
Into celestial light.

Easter Day, 2020

WHITE LIGHT

White light
Fragrance
Wafts
Acacia blossom
Through warm air.

White light
Chestnut candles
Shine out
Over a canopy of green leaves.

White light
Emanating
Into dark night,
A tiny glow-worm
Beacon signal
Gleams.

White light
Flashes
From the sword of spirit,
Pierces through
Murky veils
Into the fearless heart of truth.

White light
Scatters sacred sparks of hope,
Kindles the fiery heat of love,
Awakens seeds rising fiercely,
Standing boldly up and out,
Heralding a New Earth.

AUTUMN PATH

Slanting light
Through bent branches
Speckles
Brown leaves
Rustling
Underfoot.

A purple crocus
Displays
Its tender beauty,
The last butterflies
Still flick lightly
In lingering warmth.

The autumn path
Leads deep underground
Into mountain stillness,
The cave of the heart,
Where new life
Patiently awaits
Its time
To rise again.

CONIUNCTIO 2020

There came a man out of the land of Yehuda, sent from the Spirit, whose name was Yeshua. In him was life, and that life was the light of humanity, the light that shines against the darkness, and never has the darkness overcome it.

Gospel of the Beloved Companion 2:1

Jupiter and Saturn
Coming together,
Moving apart
In a cosmic dance,
The pulse of life itself.

Expanding and contracting,
Rising and setting,
Ascending and descending,
Growth and decay,
Light and dark
Shading into each other.

An iron grip of
Darkness and fear
Tightens around us,
Grasping, clasping,
An all-seeing eye
Penetrating
Our innermost recesses

With prying intent,
Seeking total control,
Stifling dissent
To keep us safe and secure.

In the meantime,
The fresh water of life
Still flows freely
Into clear new crystal vases
Of trust and transparency.

Hope arises in the air,
Grounded in firm resolve,
The blazing light of truth abroad,
A flame of incandescent love
Cascades across the sky
Enlightening and illuminating
Our hearts and minds within.

Moving apart,
Coming together,
Soul and spirit,
Love and Wisdom
Interweave,
Merge in sacred marriage.

New life is born in freedom,
New healing light in peace.

And never
Shall the darkness
Overcome it.

WINTER WOODS

Uber allen Wipfeln ist Ruh (Above and beyond the summits is peace)

GOETHE

Winter woods
Breathe in
Slowly
Weaving
A tapestry of silence
Brooding softly
Over sleeping earth.

Deeply resting
Still repose
Suspended a while in time.

Spring woods
Breathe out
Green leaves,
Shoots of life;
Soaring birdsong
Sparkles into bright light
Shimmering anew with warmth.

THE FIRST WHITE LIGHT

Snowdrops
Piercing
Frozen earth,
Crisp snow,
The first white lights
Of spring
Stand humbly
Watching,
Waiting,
Unwavering –
Knowing
Life cycles
Follow on
Even as they fade and droop,
Folding back from whence they came –
A sign of hope reborn.

DELIVERANCE

Every year the Earth
Gives birth to new life –
But what about us?
Can we give birth
To a new culture,
A culture of love
A culture of wisdom
A culture of truth
A culture of justice
A culture of freedom
A culture of kindness
A culture of peace
A culture of beauty?

Or will we remain
Huddled in darkness
Trapped in fear
Stifled by control
Cowed into compliance
Cancelled by censors –
Unable to breathe freely,
Sleepwalking backwards
Into digital slavery?

Deep grief wells up –
A sense of human future lost,

Of time being short,
Earth in the balance,
Breakdown and breakthrough
Coming into view.

Will this culture of hope
Be stillborn again?
Or can we finally deliver
This new world together
With courage and love?

The Earth has long awaited
This moment of deliverance
From violence and secrecy,
From deception and evil.

The world can torture
And crucify the good
But the light of love
Endures,
Comes through –
Human hearts crack open,
The birth pangs of one humanity
Awakening oh so slowly,
Agonisingly
Emerging
From the cave of suffering
To greet the rising sun.

TIME PAST

Time past and time future
What might have been and what has been
Point to one end, which is always present

T.S. ELIOT,
Four Quartets

Here God gazed out
Through eyes long dead,
Sat in sacred silence
As winds wove
Long sounds in
Waving branches.

Pray for those departed
Who once walked here,
They too lived and breathed,
Their names now etched
Deep in stone
Where moss grows over,
Their memories echoing,
Reaching down through space,
Once more present
From distant time past.

OLD TREES, NEW MAST

Mast erected,
Trees felled –
Job done,
Advancing the speed
Of screen connection.

The oaks grew
Slowly,
Steadily,
Weathering the great storms
Of 1876 and 1999.

Then came
Men with chainsaws
Following instructions –
The trees obstructed the signal,
An obstacle to progress.
In under ten minutes,
The old oaks came crashing
Stricken and sprawled,
Another connection severed
With Earth and Life.

GREEN FLOW

Green flow
Dances
On overhanging leaves,
Streams into
Still awareness
Delicately poised
In passing time.

FOR JANE – OFF PISTE

Off piste –
SO boring
On piste,
So narrowly constricted
So safely confined.

Not for Jane,
This normal piste,
So utterly lacking
In intensity,
In speed –
The breath of life itself
Eviscerated.

High peaks,
Spacious freedom
Unbounded,
The very taste
Of infinite space
In ecstatic movement.

Perfect symmetry
Gliding downhill
Weaving tracks together,

Tightly swirling
Dynamic energy
Powerfully present,
Flashing between the pines
In pure exhilaration.

Finally,
Resting in peace,
The race run
Way beyond
The finishing post of life –
Such a blessed relief:
Free at last!

My first wife Jane was a class act on the ski slopes with her indomitable spirit and boundless enthusiasm. She passed into the other world on March 1 2022 and I wrote this poem on the day.

BAPTISM BY FIRE AND WATER

The fire of the spirit
Meets the water of life
In the furnace of those hearts
Blazing with cosmic light:
Love forging,
Fusing,
Sparks flying
Like fireworks through the air
Cascading magnificently
Into the potent human soul.

The deepest thirst
Of parched humanity
Is only slaked
By new wine
Bursting through
Rotting wineskins,
And sweeping away
The old order of corruption and control.

Spiritual yearning
Longs not
For those dry stones on offer,
But for the freshness
Of the living bread of life,
Sustaining us
To eat and stand together.

THE STILL SMALL VOICE

The still small voice
Is heard only
In deep silence,
So listen softly
To the gentle notes of your soul
Awakening you within,
Giving birth
To sacred life and love.

CULTURAL MIDWIFERY

Suddenly propelled
Out of our comfort zone
Spinning into the birth canal,
Constricting pressures
Brought to bear
Give rise to existential fear,
Spiralling headlong
Into the seeming void
As the ground gives way –
Is this birth or death?
Is there no way out or through?

In the moment of surrender
Our guardian angels
Watch intently,
Awaiting our call.

From silent mountain peaks
They see new birth ahead
While we labour and struggle
In pitch darkness
Hemming us in,
Expecting deliverance
Beyond delivery
From this iron grip
Of crushing power.

Gasping,
Spluttering,
We come up and out for air,
The Breath of Spirit
Now blow freely
Through fresh spring leaves,
Joy of hope arising on the Earth,
Laughter and birdsong resounding
Through beating hearts
Together.

REGENERATION – 1321–2021

Au bout de sept cent ans, le laurier reverdira.
After 700 years, the laurel will turn green again.

GUILLAUME BELIBASTE,
The last Cathar burnt
at the stake

The laurel wilts,
Pure love
Consumed by flames,
Reduced to ash –
The orthodox letter
Quashed the gnostic spirit of freedom,
Driven into caves underground –
The flutes fell silent.

Castles laid waste by time
Retain a sacred resonance,
Hidden seeds of spiritual spring,
The force and tide of life itself
A healing power
Now rises from the inner depths
Renewing and regenerating,
Shooting forth new growth
From dry branches,
Shining a radiant star of hope
In times of dense darkness

A piercing beauty,
A flash of truth,
A beating heart of goodness
Streaming anew through the world.

This prophecy is famous in the area where we live. Over the last few years tens of thousands of box bushes were devastated by an invasive moth, but in 2021 new shoots miraculously began to appear out of these apparently dead branches – also on the slopes of Montségur, the main Cathar stronghold captured by Albigensian Crusaders in March 1244 and where 225 Cathar initiates (parfaits and parfaites) were burnt on a huge pyre at the foot of the Pog.

LOST AND FOUND

Our deepest experience –
Being one with Love
Being one with Light
Being one with another,
Each unique
Yet rooted in One Ground
One in our essential identity –
I am you, and you are me.

Knowing deeply
Love as the Law of Being
Wisdom as the Law of Light
Truth as the Law of Freedom,
Living to serve each other,
Living to heal each other,
Living to free each other,
Restoring lost connections,
Reconnecting to the Source.

THE CHAIR OF ISIS

Water flowing
Leaves rustling
Light sparkling
Chestnuts falling
Ripe from above,
Prickles protecting
Precious fruit within.

Sitting on the sacred
Stone seat immemorial
Anchors its potent presence
In fertile earth,
An ancient goddess
Born anew
Baptised by fire.

The church chimes
Draw us back
To present time,
Roasting chestnuts,
Nourishing memories,
Subtle wisps evoked
Like distant smoke rising.

The Chair of Isis can be found in a wood above Rennes-les-Bains. Its pagan origins mean that it is now known as 'Le Fauteuil du Diable' – the Devil's Seat – but it feels like an ancient place of initiation.

DEEP TIME TRAUMA

Je est un autre

ARTHUR RIMBAUD

Few and far between
Are those who dare to dive
Deeply
Into hidden recesses,
Descending
Into the dark womb
Of nascent life
Where healing awaits.

Instead
We hold on,
Struggle on the surface,
Securely barricaded
Behind our many scars and wounds.

Traumas seep through,
Stains of suffering from deep time
Penetrating
Even the screens
Of our distracted attention.

Who knows who we really are?
Those who remember,
Who reconnect in joy,
Those who make music,
Create beauty,
Dancing
In the moment,
Enabling life and love
To flow once more.

Florence, May 2022

XON 1915

Summer grasses
Blow in the wind
Where once
The village men
Now buried beneath
Fell for France.

Overhead,
Poplar leaves rustle
In dappled evening light,
And larks sing
High in the sky
Just as they sang
All that time ago.

Below them lay
Those men stretched out,
Their lives abruptly curtailed,
Their blood frozen
Their hearts lanced,
Their families on either side
Scarred and shattered
By shrapnel.

Husbands, fathers, sons
Now fading memories
For dear ones left behind,
Photos, letters, albums
Recall their once living presence
Now departed,
Though maybe watching over –
More than just a name
Etched
On standard tombstones
Still standing to attention.

In the summer of 2022 we parked our camper van overnight in Belgium and walked up to a battlefield site where over 2,000 men perished in a battle to regain a lost position neat the frontier, This brought back memories of visiting war graves in Verdun and stories of the 1914 champagne vintage in the Marne being harvested in perilous conditions evoked by the American poet Alan Seager in his moving poem 'I have a rendezvous with death'. Also first-hand stories of the Somme described by Henry Kay (1897–1990) who went straight from Eton to the front in the summer of 1915.

SUMMER TWILIGHT

The sky sinks
Seamless
Into pale pink hues
Gathering dusk
In night calmness.

The mind settles
Soothed
In the vastness,
A beckoning glow
On the far horizon.

The nearby trees
Breathe out,
A cloak of stillness
Descends slowly,
Bestowing deep peace.

BRUCH RHAPSODY

Stretching out along a bow,
Violins and cellos interweave
Subtle lines of lilting melody,
Vibrato rising and descending,
Intoning intensities,
Modulating feelings on the strings,
Emotional textures
Dissolving and resolving
The spiritual tensions of life
Stretched out along a bow.

BLACK MADONNA

Upright She sits
In regal stillness,
Her shining bliss
Resplendent
Irradiates
Our very being
To its core of darkness.

Eyes closed,
Her presence descends
Enstatic, *
Embracing the Heart of the Grail
Rooted deep within
Her secret womb:

The silently expectant world
Awaits a truly cosmic birth.

The Child Divine
Transfigured
Transmutes
Black stone to golden glow,
Transmits his dazzling blaze,
Transfusing

Sacred blood
As healing Wine
Of Life and Love.

*descending within

BLESSING OF THE DIVINE MOTHER

May the Golden Blessing
Of the Divine Mother
Descend into my soul
And dwell within my heart.

May I be infused
With the tender Power of Her Spirit,
May I be a living channel
For Her Love and Light,
Her Beauty and Peace
In the circle of my world.

THRESHOLDS

Old men ought to be explorers
Here and there does not matter
We must be still and still moving
Into another intensity
For a further union, a deeper communion . . .
In my end is my beginning.

T.S. ELIOT,
Four Quartets, 'East Coker'

Liminal advancing age
Unfolds inexorably for all,
Inviting us to recreate
Ourselves within.

Sap can still course
Through ancient branches
Renewing every year
The evanescent shoots of life.

Unimaginable at twenty
We arrive at seventy
Wondering how and where
Our past echoes into the present.

Turning inwards to the centre of being,
Our uncarved nature beckons
To silent stillness – even peace –
Savouring the sweetness of life.

May 2022

I wrote this poem in my hammock overlooking the village where we live as a reflection for my 70th birthday.

A NOTE ON THE AUTHOR

David Lorimer, MA, PGCE, FRSA is a writer, lecturer, poet and editor who is a Founder of Character Education Scotland, Programme Director of the Scientific and Medical Network (www.scientificandmedical.net) and former President of Wrekin Trust and the Swedenborg Society (www.swedenborgsociety.org.uk). He has also been editor of *Paradigm Explorer* since 1986 and completed his 100th issue in 2019. He was the instigator of the Beyond the Brain conference series in 1995 (www.beyondthebrain.org) and has co-ordinated the Mystics and Scientists conferences every year since the late 1980s.

Originally a merchant banker then a teacher of philosophy and modern languages at Winchester College, he is the author and editor of over a dozen books, including *Survival? Death as Transition* (1984, 2017) *Resonant Mind* (originally *Whole in One)* (1990/2017), *The Spirit of Science* (1998), *Thinking Beyond the Brain* (2001), *The Protein Crunch* (with Jason Drew) and *A New Renaissance* (edited with Oliver Robinson). He has edited three books about the Bulgarian sage Beinsa Douno (Peter Deunov): *Prophet for our Times (1991, 2015), The Circle of Sacred Dance,* and *Gems of Love,* which is a translation of his prayers and formulas into English. His book on the ideas and work of the Prince of

Wales – *Radical Prince (2003)* – has been translated into Dutch, Spanish and French. His new book of essays, *A Quest for Wisdom* was published in 2021.

David is also Chair of the Galileo Commission (www.galileocommission.org) which seeks the expand the evidence base of science of consciousness beyond a materialistic world view.

In 2020 he was awarded a Lifetime Achievement Award as a Visionary Leader by the Visioneers International Network and the 2021 Aboca Human Ecology Prize. He is a Creative Member of the Club of Budapest. His website is www.davidlorimer.co.uk

www.ingramcontent.com/pod-product-compliance
Ingram Content Group UK Ltd.
Pitfield, Milton Keynes, MK11 3LW, UK
UKHW041951190726
13854UKWH00005B/1904

9 791041 505692